THE WRITERS'

WORKSHOP

WORKBOOK

BY

CHARLENE TORKELSON

ISBN-13: 978-1490423760
ISBN-10: 1490423761

INTRODUCTION

For several years I have had the great privilege of teaching a series of Writers' Workshops for those who would like to move from simply putting words on paper to the next step of publishing their work. This workbook is an outline of several topics covered in these workshops. The ideas are intended to stimulate thought and consideration for those who are interested in this process. Please use the space provided to note your own ideas and impressions, set goals, and create plans for this next step.

Charlene Torkelson

START AT THE BEGINNING

Most editors and published authors when asked to give advice to new writers advise them to write about that they know. So the question is what do you know?

You will find when you write about something you are familiar with, the writing process moves along quickly and smoothly. Make a list of all the topics and subjects that you feel you know best:

_____

_____

_____

_____

_____

_____

_____

_____

_____

_____

_____

_____

Start at the beginning. That means, where were you born? You might ask, "You mean I have to go THAT far back?" Yes, list the places you have lived or visited. Those are the places you will somehow represent in your writing whether it has to do with a memory of a place or a description — it will show up in your writing. Next to each place, describe something special or unique about it. Maybe it is a specific location or a business that makes that place famous. It could be a custom or tradition. Jazz is New Orleans, Broadway is New York, and movies are Hollywood. What is special about the places you remember?

_____

_____

_____

_____

_____

_____

_____

_____

_____

We are all shaped by the people we know and meet. Whether you write fiction or non-fiction, those people will be important to your writing. Make a list of these people and describe their characteristics. What makes them a part of your life?

_____

_____

_____

_____

_____

_____

_____

_____

_____

_____

_____

_____

_____

_____

_____

_____

_____

When I began my writing career, I took a course with the first assignment to write "My Story". So now I challenge you, if you have not written your story before, do it now. Try to keep the word count at 1,000. This is a typical word count for a magazine article. So in addition to writing about yourself, you now are limited to a typical article length.

_____

_____

_____

_____

_____

_____

_____

_____

_____

_____

_____

_____

_____

_____

_____

New writers — and old writers — often find it difficult to find an acceptable writing topic. How do we find new ideas? Sometimes it might be from a news story, from a conversation with a friend, or from a long nagging interest. One exercise you might try is the word game. Begin with one word and just list subjects that have something to do with that word. I like to start with colors. For example YELLOW might lead to other words like SUN which leads to PLANETS or SUN SCREEN or SOLAR ENERGY. Or YELLOW could lead to DAISIES or FLOWER GARDENS or WHEAT or BUMBLE BEES or RARE COINS. Then these words might lead to other subjects like HOW DO BEES INFLUENCE FOOD CROPS? Or WHERE COULD YOU FIND PIRATE TREASURE?

Start your own word chains for a great way to find your next writing topic:

-

_____

_____

_____

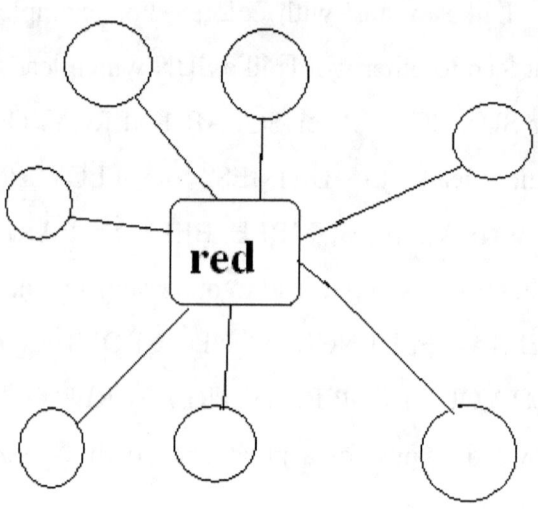

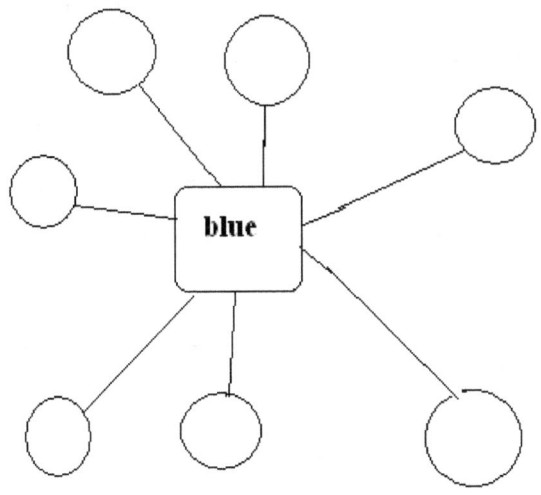

Publishers are very interested in topics that are a new or an interesting twist on a popular subject. That means you need to look outside of the box. There are several ways to do this - first, check in a book store, library or on-line to see how much is written on your topic, and second, go into your subject with a new and different approach. Editors will always reject a subject that has been written about endlessly by other authors. Give it a new twist.

_____

_____

_____

_____

_____

_____

_____

_____

_____

_____

_____

_____

_____

If you have always wanted to write that next great novel that is near and dear to your heart, begin with something smaller. In fact begin several smaller projects. The reason for this is it gives you a better chance of getting published if you submit a short story or article first. Several published articles and stories give you credibility as a writer when you actually do submit that big writing piece you really want to see in print. So make a list of short topics you could easily write. Think about an article of about 500 - 1,000 words for this.

_____

_____

_____

_____

_____

_____

_____

_____

_____

_____

_____

_____

One thing to remember, when you present your idea to a publisher, it cannot simply be an IDEA. It must be completed before you send your query. Many new writers think they are able to send out an idea without actually writing the story. Then they receive an acceptance for something that is not actually in print. They find themselves struggling to complete that idea promised to a publisher— then they have real trouble! There is nothing to send. Please, please write your article, book or story first. Then send out your query to the publishers. A great idea does not make a great manuscript!

_____

_____

_____

_____

_____

_____

_____

_____

_____

_____

_____

Now for a few cliques. Avoid "Writer's Block" by not "putting all your eggs in one basket". How is that for a few catch phrases? In other words, work on a few projects at the same time. That way when you find you are tiring or struggling with one, you are able to take a few days to work on another manuscript. When you return to the first project, you will feel refreshed and ready to tackle the issues confronting you. Sometimes the project you thought was the most marketable just isn't, and the article you didn't think was great IS. It is always best to have "your fingers in a few pots". We will end with another clique.

_____

_____

_____

_____

_____

_____

_____

_____

_____

_____

_____

As you begin your writing experience, ask yourself a few questions. Who are you as a writer? What do you want to accomplish? Define yourself. What is your vision?

_____

_____

_____

_____

_____

_____

_____

_____

_____

_____

_____

_____

_____

_____

_____

_____

_____

_____

FINDING THE RIGHT PUBLISHER

The first question I ask of the participants in my workshops is, "What is your genre?" Often times they don't know. Define your writing category. First, is it book or short article/story or poem? Is it fiction or non-fiction? Many are confused by this question. If you have written the next great novel and it is based on fact but includes conversations you as a writer imagined, it is fiction. Many fiction stories are based on truth but include details and events that are made up. Take your genre a bit further. Are you writing a picture book, board book, middle grade chapter book, adult romance, or science fiction? These are just a few of the categories you must determine. When writing children's books, you must define what age group you are writing for and that does not mean two to ten. Children's age groups are divided into many specific groups. Where does your writing fit?

_____

_____

_____

_____

It is important to determine your genre before you begin to research publishers. Each publisher has specialty genres they publish. Many new writers think a publisher is a publisher. Not so! Each has certain areas in which they specialize. It is your task to research these to discover which fit your writing. Make a list of those most appropriate for your manuscript. Use a writer's guide or check websites to find those best for your project.

_____

_____

_____

_____

_____

_____

_____

_____

_____

_____

_____

_____

_____

As you research various publishers, do not think you are the exception to their rules. If a certain publisher only works with Canadian writers and you are not Canadian, do not put them on your list. If a publisher only publishes non-fiction, they will not publish your fantasy fiction novel. Each publisher will provide a list of guidelines for writers on their website. Carefully follow these guidelines. So if they require manuscripts to be 1,000 words, do not submit 2,000 words. If they require submissions only in November, do not send yours in December. FOLLOW THE GUIDELINES.

When beginning your research, there are several areas you need to consider and note. What is the address, website, email, and editor's name? This knowledge shows the publisher when you address them that you have indeed done the research into their company. Note the % of freelancers used in a magazine, the word count requirements, submission guidelines including spacing and margins, and the topics published. What is their pay rate? Of course, the magazine or book publisher that pays the most seems to be the most appealing, but for a new writer, one that does not pay may be the best. Why? Because that may be the way to get publishing credits. Published writers are going to try for the big money. So if your goal is to get published, your first choice should be a magazine with no payment at all. Get a few published pieces under your belt before you submit the one you really want to see in print.

If you have your list of possible publishers, take a look at their websites to see what books or articles they are currently publishing. Do you like the presentation? What do their covers look like, and what other topics are they publishing? If what they do does not appeal to you, and you just can't imagine your manuscript fitting their list, do not submit to this publisher.

_____

_____

_____

_____

_____

_____

_____

_____

_____

_____

_____

_____

_____

_____

Most publishers, whether magazine or book publishers, will require a query letter. A query letter is a one page presentation of your manuscript. The first paragraph is the hook — getting the reader to continue. It gets the publisher interested in what you are writing. The second and third paragraphs give the details of the writing such as word count and reason the author wrote the manuscript. It also includes your qualifications for this writing project along with what is included in this correspondence (publishing history, resume, manuscript, etc.). The query is actually more difficult to write than your manuscript because it is short and concise. Take your time to do an excellent presentation.

_____

_____

_____

_____

_____

_____

_____

_____

SAMPLE QUERY

Publisher's name

Address

Date

Dear Editor's name,

First paragraph - intent is to get the publisher interested in your manuscript.

Second paragraph - more details about manuscript such as word count, reason for writing this piece, and qualifications.

Third paragraph - what is included in this correspondence and has this manuscript has been submitted to other publishers (simultaneous submissions). I always add a sentence explaining I am willing to make changes to accommodate their readership.

Your name

Contact info including address, email, phone number

I love researching publishers because their topics and needs always give me new ideas for my next writing project. Each year I order a Writer's Market for magazines and books. I page through to highlight the subjects I feel would be an exciting writing idea. Now I have a list of writing goals for the year. Of course I could always add to these. What topics would you find interesting? (I always keep a CURRENT Writer's Market — information in this industry changes rapidly.)

_____

_____

_____

_____

_____

_____

_____

_____

_____

_____

_____

_____

When researching each publisher, make a note of their response times. Often new writers are impatient. Remember publishers are on a different time schedule than the writer. For example, when sending in an article on Halloween, you may need to submit it by March or before to fit into the publisher's yearly time frame. So when you send in a submission, note how long it will take before you will hear from the publisher. Dates of submissions should be documented so you are aware of when it was sent and when you can expect a timely response.

_____

_____

_____

_____

_____

_____

_____

_____

_____

_____

_____

_____

I've already mentioned the phrase "simultaneous submissions". What is this and why should a writer be concerned about this term? Simultaneous submissions means you are sending a manuscript to more than one publisher. Some publishers do not allow simultaneous submissions. So when sending them your manuscript, you must wait until they have determined a "yes" or "no" before sending it on to another publisher. This can be very time consuming. Other publishers may allow a simultaneous submission **if identified**. You would identify your intent to send the manuscript to more than one publisher in your query letter. Making a publisher aware of your intent may save you an uncomfortable moment if you receive two acceptances for the same manuscript. Exciting, but uncomfortable!

Always send your manuscript in the best condition possible. Some writers feel they should be able to send a manuscript with misspellings or in a confusing format. They think the editor will look past the sloppiness. They won't. Send a query and manuscript that is top quality and very neat. If you are questioning the format for your manuscript, check a proper format for writing a paper in an English grammar book on themes. Often people tell me they understand this suggestion and then show me a manuscript that is far from an acceptable presentation.

_____

_____

_____

_____

_____

_____

_____

_____

_____

_____

_____

I have mentioned several items in connection to publishers: query, resume, outline, publishing history, synopsis, and writing samples. What are these? A query is a one page letter presenting your manuscript. A resume is your background including education and employment. An outline is a short list of what is presented in your manuscript. Publishing history lists the articles, stories or books you have had published, when and where. A synopsis is a detail of your story and what happens throughout until conclusion. A writing sample may be requested by certain publishers to see if your writing style is compatible to their publication. It may or may not be a sample that has already been published. That depends on the requirements and requests found in the publisher's guidelines.

Query_____

_____

Resume_____

_____

Outline_____

Publishing History_____

Synopsis_____

Samples_____

_____

_____

_____

_____

_____

_____

_____

_____

_____

_____

_____

_____

_____

_____

_____

_____

_____

Believe it or not, the very thing we fear — the rejection letter — may be a very effective learning tool for the writer. It gives insight into what works and what does not. For that reason when selecting publishers, make two or three lists. The first group, of course, should be your top choices. You are hoping for acceptance immediately. The second and third groups are those you will send your query to when you have received the rejections from the first group. The rejections will help you revise your query and possibly your manuscript to better fit the needs of the publisher and the reading audience.

_____

_____

_____

_____

_____

_____

_____

_____

_____

_____

One question most publishers will ask in regards to your manuscript is "Who is your market?" You need to determine who you expect your reader will be. And the answer to that question is not, "Everyone!". Then they will ask you if there are similar books or publications on your subject. Always be aware of your competition. Check with a library or bookstore to see what has already been written on your topic. Know who you are up against and what makes your idea unique.

_____

_____

_____

_____

_____

_____

_____

_____

_____

_____

_____

_____

_____

SHOW ME THE MONEY

For some people looking to move into a writing career, the prospect of being a freelancer and therefore, self employed may be confusing. It is not the usual job with the paycheck at the end of the week. Begin this new adventure by keeping very detailed records: what did you send out and to whom, what did you sell and for how much, and when can you expect to get paid. Of course, always keep track of the dates for everything. You think you will remember, but you won't. I keep a bound folder with a copy of each published article along with the cover of the magazine. We think we will remember each piece, but a few sold articles can quickly compound into many sales. Keep a record.

_____

_____

_____

_____

_____

_____

As a self employed writer, you need to be aware not just about numbers regarding writing submissions but also about finances. Keep track of sales, expenses to deduct on your taxes, and sales tax. Sales tax is a concern for those writers who sell their own books whether they are published by a traditional publisher or self-published. Make sure you check with your state on regulations and register for a sales tax identification number.

_____

_____

_____

_____

_____

_____

_____

_____

_____

_____

_____

_____

_____

Writing is just like any other career. It takes training to learn the writing business. In order to learn what is important about this career, you must take classes, read books, study, and learn. It is a never ending process especially now with this industry quickly changing. It is affected by technology and on-line publishing. It is affected by the closing of bookstores and libraries as well as the introduction of the Kindle, Nook, and ipad. So always continue to educate yourself about the craft. Take workshops and join support groups to learn the latest trends.

_____

_____

_____

_____

_____

_____

_____

_____

_____

_____

_____

Study the terms of publishing. Just what does this all mean? All rights, first rights, one time rights, second rights, kill fee. Learn the language of publishing so when you do land that big contract, you are aware of what your rights are regarding your manuscript. If you receive a contract and do not understand the terminology, take it to a lawyer that specializes in writers' contracts for clarification. Remember, you may always negotiate terms on the contract. So make a list of what may be of importance to you. Payment rates, royalties, advances, and character or photo property may be areas to consider.

All Rights:

First Rights:

One Time Rights:

Second Rights:

Kill Fee:

Royalties:

Advances:

Flat Fee:

Work-for-hire:

Be careful of contracts that indicate the publisher will have "all future rights". That means they may have rights to publishing changes in the future that we are unaware of at this point in time. Who knows what technology will be invented? A few years back we had no idea there would ever be a Kindle or Nook. It almost seemed impossible ten years ago but is quite ordinary today.

_____

_____

_____

_____

_____

_____

_____

_____

_____

_____

_____

_____

_____

_____

_____

Although we generally think of contract language for book deals, some magazines may also have a writer sign a contract. This contract is usually not quite as long and involved but may ask for a "non-compete clause". This may mean you are not able to write for a competitor. Think about this condition if you have a specific topic you would like to write about. It may limit who you are able to submit your writing to. Unless you have a wonderful relationship with the publisher you are signing this contract with, think about the implications it may have for your future as a writer.

_____

_____

_____

_____

_____

_____

_____

_____

_____

_____

Payment for writing can vary greatly depending on what is written and who is publishing that writing. There are some magazine and newspaper publishers that do not pay at all. Why would this be a good thing? A writer just starting out with no publishing history may want to get a few pieces published before sending in an important piece. Other terms to understand are: flat fee, advance, royalty, payment per word, payment on acceptance, and payment on publication. Always keep track of what your payment agreement is and when you can expect a check. There are times I have had to follow up on payments I was to receive only to discover they were missing a critical piece of information needed to send that check. Follow up on the money.

_____

_____

_____

_____

_____

_____

_____

Never think you will make a living by publishing one book. Writing involves many published books or articles. Look at the whole picture and plan several writing projects. These will begin to accumulate to give you a viable part-time or full-time writing career. This may mean looking into other options such as editing, teaching, and staff writing. Look outside the box for areas you may not have considered such as movie or book reviews, newspaper columns, greeting cards, puzzles and poems. Many writers have found these areas bring in a great deal of income.

_____

_____

_____

_____

_____

_____

_____

_____

_____

_____

_____

_____

Even if you work with a traditional publisher, it is important to promote your own work. This may be in the form of book signings, interviews with local or national television or news shows, newspaper articles, or bylines in other publications. Do not be afraid to promote yourself. Call libraries or book stores to make sure they are carrying your book or magazine. Tell family and friends about your writing. Get out there and stand on your soap box about a special published piece or book. You are your own best form of advertising. Do not think writing does not entail selling. It is all selling starting first with the acceptance by a publisher or agent. You are immediately selling your writing. Then you are again selling when your manuscript is finally published. Now you are selling your reader. I personally put together media packets for my books to send out to newspapers, television, and bookstores. It works! You need to be your own best fan.

_____

_____

_____

_____

_____

As a self employed person, you are also your own boss. That means you may write about what you choose, send out to whomever you choose, and give yourself a raise. Yes, give yourself a raise. You may do that by beginning to submit to publishers who pay more. Generally, publishers offer a wide range of payment. They might say they pay for example from $100 - $300 for an article. That gives them the flexibility to offer more money to writers who they want to continue working with on a longer term basis. They are able to raise the rate of payment to someone with whom they have developed a relationship. It may be very worthwhile to develop that relationship with a publisher right from the start to reap the financial benefits later on.

EDITING

After you have written an article, story or portion of a book, set it aside for a day before going back to edit what you have written. It allows your mind to move into a different place. When you reread something you have just written, it always sounds great because you are in the same state of mind when you first wrote the words. But a day or two later, you may think, "What did I mean to say there?" You are in a different thought process that allows you to see something in a different mindset.

_____

_____

_____

_____

_____

_____

_____

_____

_____

_____

_____

When editing, read your writing out loud. Those of us who are fast readers see the content of the message rather than each individual word and may miss an "a" or "and" because we imagine it is there. Reading out loud means we must see each and every word as we go through the sentences allowing us to catch our small but important mistakes.

_____

_____

_____

_____

_____

_____

_____

_____

_____

_____

_____

_____

_____

_____

I know that one of my writing faults is spelling. My mother used to take letters I wrote home, correct the spelling errors, and send them back to me. I realize this problem and try to be very careful about spelling mistakes. We have become too accustom to helps like Spellcheck to catch our errors. But Spellcheck is not perfect. It will not pull up a word if it is an actual word. For example, if you meant to use "your" and put in "you", it will not notify you of the mistake. So go through your manuscript carefully without assuming your computer program will catch the problems.

_____

_____

_____

_____

_____

_____

_____

_____

_____

_____

As you read through your manuscript, change any words you find yourself using over and over again. Duplicate words tend to make the writing boring. Also take out unnecessary words. I find I use the word "that" when it is not needed. So for me it is taking out ~~that~~ whenever possible. For example, "She said that it was important." If I take out "that", it becomes cleaner. "She said it was important." Much better.

_____

_____

_____

_____

_____

_____

_____

_____

_____

_____

_____

_____

_____

Writers are different. Many writers write long cumbersome sentences and when editing must cut out the unnecessary. Others write bare bones. They put down the most important parts of the story and when editing must go back and fill in — fatten the story a bit by adding more details. Which kind of writer are you? The cutter or the fattener?

_____

_____

_____

_____

_____

_____

_____

_____

_____

_____

_____

_____

_____

_____

To make an article or story more interesting, make your sentences different lengths. Some writers use "run on sentences" — sentences that go on and on forever. I used to work for a man who wrote his own advertisements for the product he invented. He could write one sentence that took up one whole page of advertising. I offered to edit his writing, but he felt he wrote extremely well . . . Don't make this mistake in your writing. Vary your sentence length. Some sentences may be longer and others short and to the point. It makes the writing more interesting.

Vary the start of your sentences. Sometimes begin with a noun and then start the next sentence with a phrase. It makes reading so much nicer. I was working with one writer on her manuscript and discovered she began each sentence with an "ing" word. When I pointed this out to her, she was surprised. It was something she hadn't noticed before. Check your writing for such habits. Starting sentences the same way is very common. Vary the start of your sentences.

_____

_____

_____

_____

_____

_____

_____

_____

_____

_____

_____

_____

_____

Just like the first paragraph of a query letter draws the editor into reading on, the opening paragraph of your book or article must draw in the reader. It is the hook of your writing. Start with something that catches the attention and makes the reader want to read more. When writing a book, a great writer does this with each chapter opening. They also end each chapter with a reason to continue to the next chapter. It is sort of a cliff hanger in book form. Hint, imply, or give a brief glimpse into what is going to happen. It makes the story so much more interesting. Always remember when writing, if you have no problem, you have no story. Story is based on conflict — an issue to be dealt with or resolved.

_____

_____

_____

_____

_____

_____

_____

_____

_____

Check on punctuation. Writers are always unsure of when to put in that comma and when to leave it out. How should the sentence end? If you are unsure, look up punctuation rules. Proper punctuation makes a huge difference in the way a story or book is read. It is also very distracting to a reader when writing is not properly punctuated. Please, if you are not sure, look it up. Also check on the proper use of some of the shorter words such as "to", "two", and "too". We all misuse these even when we know the difference. I always tell the story of a response I received from a school superintendent after I sent him a thank you e-mail. He responded with, "Your welcome." If you are reading this and don't understand what is wrong with the sentence, look it up! Remember, this was from a school superintendent! We all make mistakes.

to, too, two:

there, their, they're:

who's, whose:

its, it's:

accept, except:

capital, capitol:

where, wear:

whether, weather:

for, four, fore:

weigh, way:

Rules for commas:

_____

_____

_____

_____

_____

_____

_____

_____

_____

_____

_____

_____

_____

_____

_____

_____

_____

Carefully check your verb tenses. If you begin telling your story in the past tense, you can't insert a sentence in the middle that is in the present tense. Ask yourself from what perspective is this story told — past, present or future? Then remain consistent. The same is true for who is telling the story. Are you telling this in the first person — your point of view — by saying "I", or are you telling this in the third person? If you begin through the eyes of one character, it may be difficult to change to another character's viewpoint. Some authors will write one chapter as told by one character and the next from someone else. Be careful. I read one manuscript told by the main character when suddenly one paragraph was inserted from the viewpoint of another person. It was just one paragraph! That made the flow very confusing. So carefully check your verbs and your story perspective.

When I speak to writers about the proper format for sending in a manuscript, they all nod their heads as if they know just what I am saying. Then I look at their presentation and realize they have no idea what proper formatting is for a manuscript. Always follow the guidelines required by the publisher, but generally most will expect a Word document with 12 point font in Times New Roman double spaced. Some will give other instructions as well as margin requirements. Follow what is expected. Some may have a detailed inch requirement for the placement of the title on the page, etc. Many will tell you how to number the pages. The two most common requirements for this would be a page number centered on the bottom of the page or in the upper left corner with the author's name and title of the manuscript on each page. Many book publishers receiving longer length manuscripts may require the name and title on each page.

_____

_____

_____

_____

_____

Here is a sample format for a manuscript:

Author's name
Address
Phone
Email

Date   Word count

Manuscript Title

Body of the manuscript. . . . .

_____

_____

_____

_____

_____

_____

_____

_____

_____

_____

_____

_____

If you noticed, the sample for manuscript formatting included a space for word count. Generally the accepted wording of this is "About _____ words" even if you know the exact number of words in your article. Most publishers will give you either a specific word count requirement or an approximate length. When specific, follow the requirement. It is usually acceptable to have a 10% leeway either shorter or longer than the requirement. If the word count is 1,000 words, please do not think your article of 2,000 words will meet the requirement. You are not the exception to the rule! Follow the guidelines.

_____

_____

_____

_____

_____

_____

_____

_____

_____

_____

_____

Be consistent. If you begin to capitalize certain terms or words in your manuscript, follow through with your rule throughout. Let's talk about names. When you refer to "my mom" or "my sister" in a story, it is not capitalized. But if you use the word as a name, for example, "I told Mom I would do it.", you are using "Mom" as the person's name. It should be capitalized. If you write out your numbers, then always write them out. Don't use "10" in one place and "ten" in another. If you spell a name one way in the first sentence, don't change the spelling further down in the story. Be consistent with whatever rule you are following.

FINISHING YOUR PROJECT

We all reach a point in writing when we just can't get that manuscript finished! How can you motivate yourself to finish and move beyond the procrastination? Begin by setting some goals for yourself. I use a pie — eight pieces in a circle with a different generic heading in each piece. The circle is significant because when we have problems or issues in one of our "pieces", it affects the entire pie and not just that "piece". The eight headings I use for goal setting are: Spiritual, Career, Financial, Health/Fitness, Relationships/Family, Education, Recreation/Hobby, Environment. Under each heading, I set five goals — three short term and two long term. Without the short term goals, we never reach the long term goals. They are the stepping stones to what we really want to achieve. I try to review and renew my goals every three to six months. Goals are the road map to our destination.

_____

_____

_____

_____

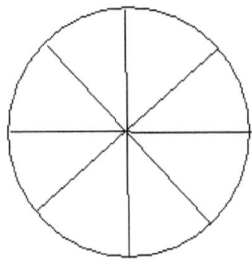

SPIRITUAL:

_____

_____

_____

_____

_____

CAREER:

_____

_____

_____

_____

_____

FINANCIAL:

_____

_____

_____

_____

_____

HEALTH/FITNESS:

_____

_____

_____

_____

_____

RELATIONSHIPS/FAMILY:

_____

_____

_____

_____

_____

EDUCATION:

_____

_____

_____

_____

_____

_____

RECREATION/HOBBY:

_____

_____

_____

_____

ENVIRONMENT:

_____

_____

_____

_____

_____

One goal for a writer that encourages completion of a writing project is to set a writing schedule. Pick your writing time or days and determine when and for how long you will be working on your writing. Creating a writing habit can be very helpful.

_____

_____

_____

_____

_____

_____

_____

_____

_____

_____

_____

_____

_____

_____

_____

A great goal for the Environment category is to create a space for yourself to write. It is so much easier to feel comfortable and begin to write when you are in an atmosphere that is conducive to creativity. I find if I have a space where I have all of my tools set up to write, I will sit down and do it. But if I have to take out what I need and put it back afterward, I am not as likely to sit down in the first place. I can find so many excuses when the place I write is not easy to use.

Along with setting writing goals for yourself, set deadlines. Give yourself a time frame in which to work. You will find publishers give out lots of deadlines. They are also very eager to work with writers who adhere to the deadlines. I always finish and submit my assignments ahead of the deadline to allow time for editing and changing parts if need be. Because I am always so dependable, I have received many additional assignments from editors who appreciate my punctuality.

_____

_____

_____

_____

_____

_____

_____

_____

_____

_____

_____

_____

If you need a little jumpstart to complete a writing project, take a class, read a self-help book, or ask for help from a fellow writer. Use the tools available to you to give yourself additional motivation. We all need a little boost from time to time. Join a writers' support group for a weekly (or monthly) pump up. As with any career, additional research and information always gives a different perspective.

No matter what you are doing, whether it is writing or something else, you will always do better when feeling your best. That may mean getting enough rest, healthy eating, and exercise. So under the Health/Fitness pie piece, reviewing your lifestyle for a few changes toward healthier living can greatly help with your motivation and productivity in writing. Consider some of the areas you might want to improve.

_____

_____

_____

_____

_____

_____

_____

_____

_____

_____

_____

_____

_____

Find someone to edit your work. I really recommend not asking a good friend or relative. They will always tell you how wonderful your writing is (unless you have the negative relative who never finds anything good about anything anyone else does!). They will love you and your work no matter how bad it might be. Ask someone else to edit for you to get honest feedback. You may have to pay a few dollars, but it is worth it. When submitting to an agent or publisher, however, never pay a "reader fee", but you may have to pay a minimal fee to someone who does editing before the manuscript is sent off. It is a good investment.

_____

_____

_____

_____

_____

_____

_____

_____

_____

_____

Some writers edit and edit and edit . . There is a point when you should stop editing and just accept that it is done. Remember, nothing is ever perfect. No matter how much you edit, there will always be something that can be changed to make it better, but if you don't move on to the next step, you won't have the opportunity to get to the publishing phase of writing. Accept that your writing is not perfect and move on. Go on to the next writing project.

_____

_____

_____

_____

_____

_____

_____

_____

_____

_____

_____

_____

_____

Goals we make are changeable. They are not set in stone. So if something you are doing is not working, change it. Review your goals and revise them for any adjustments that may be needed. Don't keep hitting your head against the wall over and over again. Go in a different direction. It is all right to change.

TRADITIONAL PUBLISHING
OR
SELF-PUBLISHING?

A few years ago, I would never advise writers to try anything but a traditional publisher. Then I began to read about experiences by other writers who recommended self-publishing and decided to look into it myself. Self-publishing has become very popular recently and seems to be the future for many writers. Both paths have their pros and cons. So take a look and decide for yourself which way is best for you. Maybe both are good choices.

Just a brief explanation, this section is related to BOOK publishing. While it is possible to self-publish your own magazine or newspaper, right now the self-publishing question is more controversial in the book publishing field.

_____

_____

_____

_____

_____

_____

Traditional Publisher

Pros:

Many writers like to focus on the writing portion of this business and leave the promotion and formatting to the publisher. The traditional publisher will design your cover and format the interior of your book as well as provide media attention for your book. This is not to say you will not do some of the promotion — you will! But you need not do as much of this with a traditional publisher. The publisher will also suggest editing ideas for you. Of course, the traditional publisher is still accepted as a standard of excellence in the writing field. Because anyone can self-publish, readers may still feel the quality work will be produced by a traditional publisher who weeds out the writers who don't quite make the mark.

_____

_____

_____

_____

_____

_____

Cons:

Basically there are two negatives about the traditional publisher. First, you may not have as much say in what the finished project will look like. Some writers really want to have their fingers in all areas of their writing project because it is so much a part of them. Second, you must also share the profits from the sale of your book. So while using a traditional publisher may get your book more exposure, and therefore, more sales, you must split the money with the publisher.

_____

_____

_____

_____

_____

_____

_____

_____

_____

_____

_____

Self-Publishing

Pros:

A few years ago, the self-publishing companies required writers to heavily invest in publishing a book. The writer had to come up with a bit of cash up front to finance the printing of the books and guarantee a large quantity would initially be printed. Today however, self-publishing does not require ANY up-front cash. The printing is done on demand and feels much like a traditional publisher would print a book. The writer, although able to hire someone from the publishing company to format, edit and design the cover, also has the option to do this work himself/herself. The writer who really wants to get personal with a manuscript is now able to do all of the designing, formatting, cover, and promotion of that book. There are those who really benefit from this. Those who are teaching a class or speaking at seminars and want to provide a book for that event is very able to do this without splitting profits with a publisher. So there is the possibility with work to make more money from this option.

There are authors who do not want to wait for a book to get picked up by a traditional publisher. It is a timely process sometimes. Then again, there are authors who will never be picked up by a traditional publisher because their writing needs work or might be about a controversial topic that a traditional publisher hesitates to chance. These authors find self-publishing the only way to go.

_____

_____

_____

_____

_____

_____

_____

_____

_____

_____

_____

_____

_____

_____

_____

Cons:

When you must wear all of the hats — writer, editor, designer, formatter, and promoter — it can be overwhelming and time consuming. Not many people are able to do it all pieces of a project with excellence. This is a decision a writer who selects this path must decide.

_____

_____

_____

_____

_____

_____

_____

_____

_____

_____

_____

_____

_____

_____

_____

SELF-PUBLISHING TIPS

Let's first look at the basic appearance of your book. If you are writing your manuscript in Word, you must first realize the way you present your book is exactly the way it will look in print. The magic book fairy will not come along and zap your book into an acceptable form. You must do that yourself. First, determine the size of your book. Most books are not the standard 8 ½ X 11 that Word uses (not to say it can't be). There are several Standard sizes as well as several Custom sizes to choose for your completed book.

Standard Trim
5.5 X 8.5
6 X 9
6.14 X 9.21
7 X 10
8 X 10
8.5 X 8.5
8.5 X 11

Custom Sizes
5 X 8
5.06 X 7.81

5.25 X 8
6.69 X 9.61
7.44 X 9.69
7.5 X 9.25
8.25 X 6

When you have determined what size will work for your book concept, resize your book in Word to see how many pages your manuscript will now be when printed. Remember when resizing to consider the margins as well. The print may need a different sides, top and bottom adjustment to look the way you want it to when printed. The number of pages will determine the print cost of your manuscript into book form. So if you have a thousand page novel, you will have quite a hefty print cost. You will also select what price you will be charging for your book, and this is based on the cost to print. So if your epic novel costs too much, your reader will not purchase your book. Set a few price points you would like to use as a guideline so you can make any changes while editing to fit that framework. I noticed with one self-publisher the authors were pricing their books very high. While a higher price will give you more money from a sale, it may also limit how many sales you have. Weigh the pros and cons of each — higher price and more royalty or lower price and more books sold. Which works for you?

_____

_____

_____

_____

_____

_____

_____

_____

_____

_____

_____

_____

_____

_____

_____

_____

_____

Your cover, both front and back, will also need to fit the size you have chosen for your print page. After you have completed your writing and formatting, determine the number of pages your book will be including title page, copyright page, introduction, table of contents and any blank pages needed to allow your book to open to a first page on the right side. These are all included in your page count. Then submit this count to your publisher along with the page size to print out a cover template. The template will give you the dimensions you will work with to design your cover. This template will give space for the front cover, back cover and spine. Using a publishing program such as Publisher or GIMP, insert your cover designs along the template guidelines and determine how you want your spine to look. Then save this as a Word file and again as a PDF file. The PDF file is the one you will upload to your publisher's site. The inside portion of your manuscript should also be saved as a PDF file and uploaded.

_____

_____

_____

_____

When typing and planning the hard copy of your book, consider what you may need to do to convert this book to an ebook. At this time, the various popular ebooks are in different formats. It would be so much easier for writers who would like to format their manuscripts themselves if this would change in the future. I predict it will. While I do not profess to be any type of expert at all in computers, formats, and programs, I did format several of my books myself — with the help of a few of my college aged children I had to beg for assistance. Our generation is not as knowledgeable as the younger generation who has grown up with the technology of today. It is not an easy process, I will confess. Some of the type and spacing of the Word file does not easily transfer to ebook format. These things are quickly changing, and the transition is becoming easier and easier. I have noticed some symbols do not transfer, and it is not advisable to use your Tab key to indent paragraphs as it doubles the spacing in the transfer.

_____

_____

_____

_____

SHOULD YOU FIND AN AGENT?

People usually ask about finding an agent. While many writers will tell you it is important to have an agent, I am a little reluctant to advise a new writer to immediately find an agent. The process to find an agent is about the same as finding a publisher. You must submit your manuscript, query, and publishing history/resume to an agent just as you would to a publisher. There are some genres that really do need an agent. Adult fiction novelists will find an agent does generally have more connections to some of the larger publishing houses. Also consider if you use an agent, you once again split your profits with another group, and you are already splitting your money with the publishing company. An agent is great for better connections and should be able to get a better contract. If the agent doesn't do this, then they are not needed. The best agents are already representing enough writers that they do not need anyone new in their stable. So most new authors looking for an agent will most likely find a newer agent as well. This is one area you might want to consider the pros and cons before jumping in. SCBWI (Society for Children

Book Writers and Illustrators) offers lists of agents on their website for their members. They also provide legal answers and connections to illustrators, writing contests, and grants. I highly recommend looking into membership in the SCBWI.

Just a quick last note on agents. If they charge a reading fee, find someone else. Be very careful to find an honest and reputable agent. There are many who are not.

COMMENTS ON OTHER TOPICS

Writers designing picture books always ask about illustrations and illustrators. You do not need to provide an illustrator (or illustrations) if you are submitting copy to a publisher. In fact, most publishers recommend an author not do so unless they are also an artist. Publishers have favorite illustrators they like to use for their books. If you are an artist, you may also consider submitting a portfolio or sample illustrations to publishers to keep on file for use in their upcoming book projects.

_____

_____

_____

_____

_____

_____

_____

_____

_____

_____

_____

Picture book writers should also understand what a "mock-up" or dummy is. Picture books are usually printed in a format that looks like a page folded in half. That means there are certain standard page counts used in this process. Generally they are 16, 32 or 48 page formats. Remember, included in this page count is the title page, copyright page, and any dedication page as well as blank pages. Many publishers will request you submit a mock-up indicating where you want your copy and your illustrations.

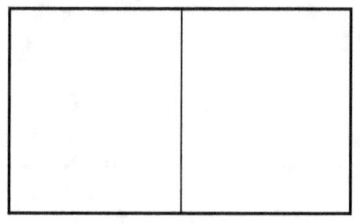

This is a sample mock-up page. If you took 8 of these pages and fold them, you would have the 32 page format. On each page indicate where you want your words and pictures.

_____

_____

_____

If you are considering self-publishing a book, determine before you publish what your promotion plan will be. How will you get your book out in front of your readership? Currently writers are using several methods: google and other search engines, facebook, Pinterest, Linkedin, blogs, and Twitter. Most writers will also recommend having a website to promote their product(s). Have these options in place before you complete your publishing process so you are able to immediately send out information to your readers. That may mean establishing a following before you put out the book. Connect with a lot of people! Who do you think your readership will be?

Other items to consider are business cards to distribute, media packets, and fliers. You might consider contacting retail stores you think would be interested in displaying your book. Think outside the box on this one. For example, if you write about plants, consider offering your book for sale at greenhouses or florist shops. Having said this, please make sure you publish a hard copy at the same time as you put out an ebook. While ebooks are gaining popularity among readers of all ages, you must have something physical in hand when promoting your book.

Although I don't like to show favoritism toward certain companies or products, I will tell you who I personally use for some of these areas. I recommend finding your own favorites as well.

Amazon.com

Barnes and Noble

Createspace (self-publisher owned by Amazon)

KDP Select (Kindle publisher)

Wordpress (for bloggers)

Goodreads

Vistaprint (FREE business cards and other supplies)

Facebook

SCBWI (Society for Children's Book Writers and Illustrators) a wonderful group for writers of all genres

www.writersbookstore.com They publish writer's market books both for books and magazines.

The Institute of Children's Literature A great place to take correspondence writing classes and workshops.

Register.com for websites

This list is only a start. There are many other places to consider in your promotion process. Ask other writers who they use for media services.

_____

_____

_____

_____

_____

_____

_____

In my workshops, I always tell writers to contact me with questions. So I will end with this as well — contact me!

Charlene Torkelson

TCTork@msn.com

www.chartorkelson.com

Or find me on Facebook, Twitter, Pinterest or Linkedin.